BYLINES 'ROUND THE EYES

*Who I am and
all I've known,
engraved experience
on a fleshy pallet,
those bylines
'round my eyes.*

───────────

ANN EVERETT

ANN EVERETT

Copyright © 2009 Ann Everett

ISBN 978-0-9822543-3-2

Cover Art and Illustrations

by Ann Everett

All rights reserved. No part of this book may be reproduced or transmitted in any form or by any means electronic or mechanical, including photo copying, recording, or by any information storage and retrieval system without written permission from the copyright owner.

Tanos Books
publishing

1110 West 5th Street
Coffeyville, Kansas 67337

Printed in the United States of America

PREFACE

Poems are blessings, each one birthed and given permission to develop its own personality. The poet places words on the page; but, the poems seemingly exist as a product of their own invention.

The creative process is exciting and grueling. Perhaps this is because each poem is an example of the voices living inside the author's skull. Poems dance, sing, sulk, or demand justice.

Sharing poems is quite different from sharing most prose. The mind, spirit, humor, and history of the author are exposed to the world.

My word-children (poems) remind me of my humanity. I hope readers identify with a few of them. Oh, the power of word kinship.

ANN EVERETT

THIS BOOK IS DEDICATED TO MY HUSBAND,

BOB EVERETT

TABLE OF CONTENTS

KANSAS AND NATURE
Kansas ...11
Telling Time ...13
The Band Concert ...15
Asibikaashi ...17
Small Town Women ...19
Trees ...21
Columbus Day ...22
The Buffalo ...23

HUMOR AND LIGHT VERSE
Aerobics ...27
Space Challenged ...29
Paisley ...30
Poppyseed Child ...31
Rorschach ...33
Granola Bars ...34
Election ...35
Problem Solving ...36
Right Brain—Left Brain ...38
Writing Class ...39
Bookworm, Bookworm, Where Are You? ...40

ANN EVERETT

AGING
Forever Young …45
Ashes to Ashes …46
Haiku …48
Solstice …49
Middle Ages …50
The Dance …51

THE BYLINES 'ROUND MY EYES
Maternal Instincts …55
The Bath …57
Haiku …59
The Gift of Now …60
In the Language …62
Wind Tossed …64
The Second Date …65
Impatient ,,,67
There Was Masada …68
Sandman …70
Advent …71

MUSIC
jazz … 75
the organ …76
Here Comes J. D. …77
Klezmer …79
His First Solo …80

QUESTIONING
    The Affected ...83
    A Conversation With Kings ...85
    In The Beginning ...87
    This Is The Way It's Always Been Done ...89
    The Dichotomy Of God And Godliness ...90
    Nothing New ...91
    The Hospital Grill and Deli ...92
    Blue Shadows ...93
    Stalactites ...94
    I Am Woman ...95

LAST GOODBYES
    A Visit From A Stranger ...99
    Breastplates ...102
    The Corridor ...103
    Goodbye ...104
    I Just Love You ...105

THOSE I HAVE KNOWN
    Christmas ...109
    The Caretaker ...110
    Perfection ...112
    Graduation ...113
    Skywriters ...114
    The Poet's Baptism ...115
    The Pact ...116
    A Two-Year Old Christmas ...118

FAMILY
    Eighteen ,,,121
    Collision Course ...122
    Angel Wings ...123
    Winter Storm ...125
    I Hold My Breath ...128
    Unconditional Love ...131
    Heritage Web ...132

MOTHER
    Finding Voice ...135
    The Spice Shuffle ...136
    Behind The Lines ...138
    Circle Of Life ...139

WOMEN'S/CHILDREN'S ISSUES
    The Price of Bread ...143
    Depression ...145
    Love Children ...146
    A Woman's Commute into the City ...147
    Wait Here ...148
    Silent Screams ...149
    Bagatelle ...151
    From A Forty-Nine Plymouth ...152
    Rebecca ...153

KANSAS AND NATURE

ANN EVERETT

KANSAS

Grand, brown woman,
  salt water bathed,
    tidal wave charged,
      shell and creature
        washed into her pores.
Prismed crystals
  of the ice gods
    fingered and forged
      a sculpted matron—
        scape touching sky.
Wind whipped Kansas;
  violent whirls ripped
    away bush and tree,
      her apparel.
        zephyrs consoled her.
Lady Kansas
  smiled at the wind
    and nurtured another
      seedling—remedy
        for bruises and scars.

ANN EVERETT

Kansas bore the world
  zealots and statesmen,
    artists and dullards,
      natives and explorers.
        She mothered them all.
We from her belly
  stood on her chest
    admiring her wholeness.
      With our hands on her heart,
      she completed us.
And if we stood
  long enough on
    any rise, we could see
      Kansas, the terra firma
      of time, breathe.

TELLING TIME

The poet tells time
by ode or limerick
and the novelist
pieces together time
chapter by chapter.

Writers of history
teach our children
"the time of..."

when the buffalo
walked the plains...

when the Native Americans
lived in tribal villages...

when White Man came...

when Kansas became a state...

when our first astronaut
journeyed into space.

ANN EVERETT

Buffalo run through time,
the chapter read and reread
with fluidity and
without the reverence
given sand falling
through the hourglass.

Native American issues
trapped in book bindings—
past glories in analytical paragraphs,
facts colder than Kansas winters in predawn—
are relegated to fine type and lithograph.

Spinning tales inside time frames
as rigid as pocket watch gold,
limits the continuum
trailing into the future
on the heels of buffalo,
Native Americans
and space travelers.

THE BAND CONCERT
The 1950's

Between gold fields of blowing grain
and cattle still in pastures green,
a farming town dots rolling plain
and highway four cuts serpentine
across six blocks of tree lined Main.

The town of Hope on Saturday night
becomes alive with Sousa, Key,
quick march songs, show tunes, notes in flight
o'er ladies serving coffee, tea,
and homemade ice cream 'neath starlight.

The bandstand light fades into black
where children capture fireflies mild
in jars with punctured lids. A sack
of saved, new pennies grant the child
a "two- or three-for" candy snack.

ANN EVERETT

Shrill screams of girls tormented by
young boys with locusts loosely held
beginning chase of those so shy.
High water tower, red cap shelled,
above the roof tops touches sky.

While men on benches talk of wheat
and livestock prices, up or down,
on wooden floor planks women meet
acquaintances and shop uptown
for something, nothing, just retreat.

The silence after closing shops
returns the village to the plains,
coyote wails, train whistle-stops,
bright stars and moon through windowpanes,
gray field mice, windmills, growing crops.

ASIBIKAASHI

Giizis means sun. Asibikaashi—Spider Woman.
The dream catcher numbers eight points
for Spider Woman's eight legs.

Giizis falls. Red, cumulous clouds hem the sky
as oak embers glow after a sweet pine blaze.
In the lodge a brown child flails,
breath and limb in unsynchronized choreography.

Dreams stir.
The mountain lion of the child's invention
becomes a wily pack;
saliva-coated, yellowed teeth bear
and hungry eyes flash;
human existence fragile before the foul breath
of decaying meat.

The child's fear and his shame of the fear—
the innate and the learned.
What is to be conquered and the invincible
engage the dream.

ANN EVERETT

> The lions grow heavier and taller,
> draw closer as fear diminishes him.
> Growls inspire a quickened heartbeat.
> Terror pours from his skin,
> drenching yellowed bed sheets.

The child's fear dances in the lions, soars above cliffs,
masks itself inside mange, grime and primitive curses.
Each time the child turns away the head-pictures follow.

Dreams no longer pulsing, dancing or soaring,
feed the light in Asibikaashi's web.

SMALL TOWN WOMEN
Written for the Domestic Science Club
Herington, Kansas

Some women wear a small town
the way a broad-shouldered
movie star wears mink—
        trailing
                over her
                        shoulder—
or in a manner reminiscent
of the flamboyant aunt
who scandalized corseted women
        one-hundred
             years
                    ago.
Other women are rooted,
blooming again and again,
like crocus in early March—
        yellow
            magic
                on a white pallet,
those staid ladies who volunteer
for this or that, tend gardens,
play cards and bake pies
        without
            Mrs. Smith
                or Sara Lee.

ANN EVERETT

Beyond shared gossip, they know
who came from where and whose daddy
drank too much or whose mother acted as a midwife—
        local
                history
                        in perfect recall.
As women always have done, sod house
to the white frame cottage, they cry together,
support the frail, admire each other's grandchildren,
        and laugh
                and touch
                        and heal.
Small town women are soul,
the music in the choir loft,
the breath and pulse of life
        along
                brick
                        streets.
Those who stay keep close to
and those who leave
take memories of
        a small town
                woman's
                      heart.

TREES

Season changes warmth to chill,
blue to gray, nest to flight.
On the dark slate of the universe,
gnarls in the branches script
the history of another passing year.
What cannot be seen are the rings—
haloes trees wear at their core,
gifts from the Creator.

ANN EVERETT

COLUMBUS DAY

Columbus flags whip red, white, blue
O'er ornamental gourds for sale.
Carved, voiceless pumpkins screaming, "Boo!"
Triangle eyes flick-flicker pale.

THE BUFFALO

Inside the dust cloud building in the west,
five hundred hooves beat and stir the prairie,

> quaking dew laden webs,
> bending prairie grasses,
> echo filling,
> echo chilling
> the not-yet-named Flint Hills.

> In static-charged fear,
> the prairie dog burrows deeper;
> a hawk flies against the sun,
> deer scatter.

Buffalo charge through an era, their reign to claim,
viewing vistas, horizon to horizon, atop terra rolls

> before the buffalo have enemies,
> before the greedy hunters,
> before the slaughter,
> before a nickel head
> reduces creatures to wet palms.

ANN EVERETT

HUMOR AND LIGHT VERSE

ANN EVERETT

AEROBICS

"Begin with a one-twenty beat.
Grapevine right. Grapevine left."

I watch myself move in the mirror;
a hot blush rises up my neck and
perspiration seeps through my tee.
Grind and grunt. I hear, "Suck it in.
Shoulders back. Lift those knees.
Punch it. Push."

 "Time to increase the beat."
At one-seventy-eight
we dance off cake and pie,
supreme pizzas, sundaes,
fried meat, every treat.

The leader cools down,
her endorphins all aglow.
I cling to the thought,
It's a miracle I'm alive!

ANN EVERETT

The slow down—
"Inhale. Exhale.
Stretch it out. Relax."
My guru gives kudos
and little mints by the door.

When I return nothing will change—
the instructor's words, my red face,
or the pumping of my steam engine heart.
Fitness dreams are hard to kill.

SPACE CHALLENGED

A mind journey into the world
of space-challenged words
began in Wartrace, Tennessee.
Words flew past the car window.
Was it War Trace or Wart Race, Tennessee?
Does Gingrich posses property in Newtown (Newt own)?
Does the choir in Gladstone (Glads tone), Michigan
outshine the one in Grindstone (Grinds tone),
Pennsylvania?
When Gladstone and Grandstone records music
is the process called loadstone (loads tone)?
Do elk live in Fawnskin (Fawns kin), California
and read the Rampage (Ram Page) Chronicle?
What does William sport in Williamsport, Ohio?
Have I proven what a scampi (scamp I) am?

ANN EVERETT

PAISLEY

He wore a paisley tie
that caught my wild mind's eye;
repeated patterns seen
in gourds and blood red spleen,
balloons for quotes, and tears,
small apple seeds, hound ears,
one loop of knotted bow,
black spades, goat horns to blow,
eyes, breasts, the cursive "e,"
a ukulele wee,
Aladdin's magic lamp,
gold harp, a feather vamp,
and South America
or deepest Africa.
A paisley print did tease,
imagination seize.

POPPY SEED CHILD

The Poppy Seed Child
dressed a paper mache lion—
mommy's pearls fleeced the mane;
daddy's ties braided a tail.

She wore ruby-studded silks
when she mounted that lion.
The starting gates opened
and the race was on.
First through the gate was a zebra on skates,
leading a green ostrich in a three-piece suit,
and thundering last was a hundred-legged ant.

Rabbit-eared mimes, purple striped skunks
and pastel dogs applauded, howled
and began to dance; they leapt
toward the sky of two suns and six moons.

Marshmallows rained chocolate drops, cookies
and cakes—pelting the track with pastry and goo.
But determined was that Poppy Seed Child
as she and her lion outran the rest.
She was a heroine and a trophy did win
because she never gave up as she rode like the wind.

ANN EVERETT

RORSCHACH

From hundreds of patterns
I selected a pastel
for bath walls—
water color madness.

Through gritted teeth the paper hanger said,
"They'll never know the difference—
matched or unmatched seams."
Debubbled, color clung to plaster.

Alone with blue patches on pink puddles,
yellow rivers and cotton bowl whites,
I found the artist's renderings
quite pornographic.

Parted, pink legs reached toward the ceiling,
a tuft of white where they met.
Everywhere I looked, she was waiting,
blue sky between bended knees. No shame.

After my shower, I patted
my breasts, stomach and thighs dry
and wondered if she saw me
as clearly as I saw her.

ANN EVERETT

GRANOLA BARS

look like fodder,
have no smell,
crack tooth enamel,
take two weeks to digest.

insults and granola—
roughage,
chewed and rechewed,
gut wrenching.

ELECTION
For Fools and Falsehoods

Election year—any will do—
when politicians seal their fate,
campaigning hard, defining new
the phrase *the leader LIES in state.*

ANN EVERETT

PROBLEM SOLVING

Lug nuts loosened by rough roads
caused a farmer's truck to collapse
onto broken pavement.

Three congressmen stopped,
stroked their chins,
and offered political solutions.

The first concentrated
on the spoke's creation—
a perfect pie chart.

The second pulled out a hundred-dollar bill,
"Here, grease the axle with this.
It may not solve the problem,
but at least you're doing something."

BYLINES 'ROUND THE EYES

The final politician laughed and said,
"Blame your wife, the mechanic,
or any administration—past or present.
Someone will believe you if you repeat
the same message often enough."

The farmed watched
the congressmen's limo speed away.
He rescued his wheel from the ditch,
retrieved his lug wrench, and
rolled up his sleeves.
"Guess to get something done
you have to know
what you're talking about."

ANN EVERETT

RIGHT BRAIN—LEFT BRAIN

Fuzzy, white caterpillars ride
above my brows until I pencil in color.
Either the right brow arches up
forming the uppermost hook of a question mark
or lies as flat as an EKG line for the expired.
The left eyebrow stretches unnaturally over the nose,
no balance with the right brow.

Artistic flair or engineering?
Yin or yang?
Left or right brain?
What school of thought
could color and shape my brows,
bring harmony to my world?

WRITING CLASS

Close loops like springs never sprung
and wide-eyed smiley faces—
doodles on my paper suggest
a mind too vacant to compose
a poem or map the way back home.

ANN EVERETT

BOOKWORM, BOOKWORM, WHERE ARE YOU?

*What would happen if Dr. Suess wrote
for the United Methodist Women's Reading Program?
Skit written for the Salina District UMW meeting in 2000.*

ALL: Bookworm, Bookworm, where are you?

WOMAN 1: I have so much to do, to do,
    a hullabaloo, shampoo to pew.
    I coo and stew, make do,
    undo, a pebble in my shoe — phew!
    Some say I haven't got a clue,
    a venue with no follow-through.

ALL: Bookworm, Bookworm, where are you?

WOMAN 2: I'm an endorsee — not enlistee,
    a wouldn't be, couldn't be attendee.
    A devotee of my privacy,
    I can't hear the plea,
    "Open sesame."
    My psyche lodged in mind's deep sea—
    tea, no we, on my settee.

ALL: Bookworm, Bookworm, where are you?

WOMAN 3: An extrovert, each action overt,
    I flirt and spurt, flash my pettiskirt.
    I'm young and pert in my T-shirt;

BYLINES 'ROUND THE EYES

>   but I assert I too am convert.
>   Drums and keyboards now insert
>   for tomorrow's church and a new concert.

ALL: Bookworm, Bookworm, where are you?

WOMAN 4:   I'd say the young are cockeyed—
>   Untried with a style less than dignified.
>   *The-way-its-always-been-done* guide
>   has been declassified, set aside!!
>   What was bona fide does not
>   coincide unless the officers are
>   Jekyll and Hyde.

ALL: Bookworm, Bookworm, where are you?

WOMAN 5: Green eggs and ham,
>   excuse me ma'am, wrong ditharamb.
>   I am the one with the program
>   the one in a jam.
>   Took notes to my exam
>   and read them over a yam,
>   then my car door did slam — Wham!
>   Goodbye Abraham.
>   My mind a scattergram,
>   I stand here meek as a lamb.

ANN EVERETT

ALL: Bookwork, bookworm, where are you?

WOMAN 6: (spoken slowly)
    A-a-a-a-aw shucks.
        Let's get to the crux
            of the matter—we need the influx
                of more potlucks
        and less input from high muck-a-mucks
        with their nips and tucks.

BOOKWORM: What is all this gobbledygook?
        The corset unhook and take a look
        at what we took
        from Wesley and the Good Book.
        No need to make a donnybrook
            o'er what's in man's playbook.
            Any book on the UMW list—
                storybook, pocketbook,
                chapbook or guidebook—
        is a hook for a better outlook.

ALL: Thank you, Bookworm, you uncurled my perm.
    I do affirm I've caught the reading germ
        and am proud to confirm,
            I'm a UMW "heart-worm."

AGING

ANN EVERETT

FOREVER YOUNG

I sashayed to dulcet musings,
a lusty, leather shuffle across
the percussion of concrete,
sand and pebbles.

I captured and was held captive
by the stares of boys, naughty and nice,
entertaining a teen's imaginings
of what will or will not be.

Today's trade-offs: lust for wisdom,
musings for peace,
sandals for practicalities.
Untruth.

The shuffle, sounds and fantasies
waltz through the unexpected laugh,
rebel's sigh, and dreams
I dream.

ANN EVERETT

ASHES TO ASHES

A gray hair away from fifty,
half a century spent, I look forward.
Between the horizon and me lies
less time to laugh, rage and engage
than moments already wasted on things
others lay on my shoulders as "shoulds"
or offices in women's clubs,
the solace of by-laws, constitutions,
and good manners.

I cross the prairie, eager to focus
on anything short of the horizon
and become a worn pioneer
from the last century,
my car a Comstock
or mule along the Santa Fe Trail.

Birds in a straggled "V"
fly over green winter wheat.
Wind blows buffalo grass against broken fencing
and a Styrofoam cup dances across asphalt.

Where will my ashes venture on Kansas winds?
Perhaps an ash will sail onto a pond,
a water bug hovering to one side;
another ash will find harbor in a knotty fence post;
an ash will be carried on a dove's wing

BYLINES 'ROUND THE EYES

into a red-paint-peeling barn;
bits of me in a choir loft,
on a flee-ridden hound chasing butterflies,
at a little league game,
on yellow roses delivered by a florist,
or riding in a parade on a steamy, hot summer's day.

I refuse to grieve fifty. I refuse to grieve.

If, by chance, this is read after I'm gone,
remember me when the wind blows,
in a kernel of wheat,
when you smell honeysuckle,
when jazz blares,
or a computer glares in a half-lit room.

I refuse to grieve.

You refuse to grieve.

ANN EVERETT

Fifty

Graying, fraying

Too old to start over

Too young to stop living the dance

Midway

SOLSTICE

The supple and beautiful pass
as the red apple spots,
ballet legs swell,
and storm winds stir clear waters.

Gravity lowers breasts—
humility entertains memory.
Temples gray—
ashen as on a cooled volcano.

Solstice: celebration of and
resignation to the sun
balanced between rise and set,
the right foot lodged in the past
and the left toes searching
for even footing—closure,
holding on,
letting go.

ANN EVERETT

MIDDLE AGES
For Corkie Dunlap

Unfettered by slip and hose,
she eases her long-skirted, sandaled gait
and faces the mirroring of her mother.

Age is like ivy clinging midway up a brick wall—
rooted deep and rushing upward; and
age is like the flowers at a parent's funeral,
each scented petal real and the experience unreal.

Ink on birth and death certificates plays
inevitability against lullabies,
laugh lines, and errors in judgment.
Ink fades on marriage licenses, divorce decrees
and sketches kept as souvenirs
after parties and partings.

Last rites and last writes—
naming pain, exploring joy,
living the last chapter.

THE DANCE

When I was two I danced with time
around the homegrown Christmas tree.
Potbellied stove and quilts did warm
my wee socked feet once stilled for sleep.

When I was twelve I danced in time
in party dress—ruffles and lace.
A young man's hand and mistletoe
did warm my being. One-step-two.

At eighteen I became the dance
of brave new worlds, of fear not shown.
Foreboding chilled warmed innocence.
Brave one-step-two. Shy one-step-two.

At forty-five tree lights danced 'round
my memories of time and those
whose shadows followed me as ghosts
in step. Step slide. Slide step. Step slide.

At sixty-two I knew the dance;
I knew the ghosts and called them friends.
As when age two, in my socked feet
I neared the fire and stilled for sleep.

I danced through time and did become
the dance of movement, rhythm, grace.
For all we own to give or hold
is time and dance. Dance one-step-two.

ANN EVERETT

THE BYLINES 'ROUND MY EYES

ANN EVERETT

MATERNAL INSTINCTS

I was seven and wore loneliness
the way sunflowers wear October,
heads bent and color spent.

A bird's nest lay in dewy light,
a web of straw and twigs.
I pulled a feather from the nest and
brushed my cheeks with softness
like the wings of daybreak,
black velvet or lullabies.

A fledgling struggled in bladed jungle
until scooped into my hands and
proudly presented to my mother
who touched only what was clean.

The adopted bird and I were exorcised
from the tidy kitchen to avoid lice
or some unknown contamination.
The fowl, christened Tweety,
was placed back in his nest,
just as Raggedy Ann or the doll that wets
was lovingly given a place to sleep
when not held against the chest.

ANN EVERETT

Carefully, I balanced the nest
on the smokehouse sill,
the window missing since forever.
I turned up boards beside the old Ford
and harvested worms—an a la carte menu.

Thoughts of the bird in my charge
woke me from morning slumber;
I ran across wet grass to the vacant sill.
I strained to look inside the blackened
smokehouse, called and listened
for his voice—a peep, a rustle.

Inside the adult-child *Sometimes
I Feel Like a Motherless Child* still plays
and I remember my failure.
The inkwell quill in retribution boldly recalls
labeled, separated, lost souls—human or fowl—
lying on smokehouse floors,
banished from the earth.

THE BATH
The 1950's

Raindrops splattered on the tin roof,
then fell through tin pipes until they reached
the dark cistern under the porch.
The crank moved roller coaster cups
to capture water drawn to light
and spill the liquid into a metal tub.
Clickity, splash, clickity, splash, clickity, splash.
Neck veins and muscles bulged as the tub
was lifted onto the flame. Molecules danced.

A four-legged rinse tub, the receptacle
for clothes rung flat on wash day,
was rolled beside the pot bellied stove.
Once filled with water, the bath was an invitation
to the pigtailed child who made mud pies
and to her mother worn by the
oppression of daily chores
and by the activity of her smiling, pigtailed child.

ANN EVERETT

A white-chipped chair of many coats
exposed green enamel and provided the avenue
for a naked child to reach up,
over and into the rinse tub.
With a cloth and homemade soap, the grime
and blue of wild mulberries created a soup
of water, soil and pink flesh.

Raindrops given another course
might have encouraged the blush of a rose
rather than the blush
given the cheeks of the pigtailed child.

BYLINES 'ROUND THE EYES

Haiku

Each day Brutus barked

At a black snake in our yard,

Roamin' Cassius.

Large circle of sunflowers

Little green wheat field

Guacamole in yellow bowl

ANN EVERETT

THE GIFT OF NOW

A hedge row stitches suede sky to prairie patches.
I brake for a weathered, red truck
and read the "eat beef" bumper sticker.
My pulse slows as Public Radio plays
Jesu, Joy of Man's Desiring.

'Tis the season of joy and love,
the celebration of birth.
I study a cloud blowing across the sky
and feel the wind pushing my Intrepid;
the inevitability of death is not in season.

The truck stops; turns left.
I return the farmer's wave
and feel the upturn of my mouth.
A smile. Joy. Life.

Soon I will be home with a man
who does not remember past seasons,
when he ate, the date or sometimes my name—
the sum of life in the now.
He would have enjoyed the fast moving cloud.
I regret he is not with me.

BYLINES 'ROUND THE EYES

I once believed the polish of marriage
was in the memory factory;
each photo lovingly placed in an album
represented a forever reality.
When the now of yesterday is gone,
what do we cherish?

The now embraces each moment as a new birth.
A shared smile captures forever.
A cloud echoes celestial joy.
Holding hands is the all of life.

Wise men and women—farmers in red trucks,
men without memory and you, sages all—
celebrate the birth of love in a solitary cloud, a smile,
a touch in the nativity of a moment.

ANN EVERETT

IN THE LANGUAGE

Scent of pine,
bare oaks brushing sky,
fields of snow-patched winter wheat—

I listen for a phrase never spoken,
the language soft and foreign—almost French,
words outside Webster's Collegiate Dictionary,
syllables to slow my breathing,
to define ribs pushed by lungs until full;
and to reassure children, drunks,
ministers, wealthy, poor.

A cardinal feeds on winter berries;
the wind wraps a hawk in its strength;
and a child's foggy breath warms cold fingers.

I struggle to hear the pulse
of words in melodic measures,
a song just beyond my hearing,
a dialogue needed to reason
footprints in snow, squirrels' chatter,
and red ice hanging from clouds.

BYLINES 'ROUND THE EYES

Deer meet at dawn beside frozen water;
pinecones and brown leaves litter forest floors.

The language is in the night,
the murmur between stars and owls,
the whisper of snowflakes,
the lonesome cries of wolves and wind.

I listen for a song—a quiet, courageous voice
spilling words never invented.

The solace: I know the mystery language I hear is real.
The joy: I make harmony with constellations,
                                    foxes and doves.
The peace: When I have no voice,
                                    the song will play on.

ANN EVERETT

WIND TOSSED

Gale force winds rip through me;
debris lashes the face and legs;
dust veils vision.

Just briefly,
I turn away in defeat,
a moment of respite.

No human dare claim the wind—
the diminished made to bow down,
ruled by the unruly.

I grab a piece of the wind,
own the power, control a stormy minute,
stuff the wind gust into my gingham pocket.
The bulge swells as I clamp
the pocket to my thigh.

Behind closed doors, I open a flattened pocket,
reach inside and finger a frayed seam.
I dare not look at the loosened threads.

I weep for the tortured wind,
for the bruise on my thigh,
for frayed seams.

No human dare claim the wind.

THE SECOND DATE
For Bob

I sat in my car and watched
my blind date enter Olive Garden.
I studied his walk, the blue, plaid shirt
and unremarkable pants—
a man in need of woman.
He did not look happy to be in that place,
meeting ME for the first time.
How could that be?

I had been to the beauty shop, done my nails,
and purchased new clothes
for my first date in over thirty-years.
Did he not realize this was an occasion?
I took a deep breath
before slipping out of my seat and
taking the long walk across the parking lot.
Mr. Blue-Plaid-Shirt might not like me.
I could survive rejection. Maybe.
I was thinking *I should have lost weight*
before throwing myself into dating; or, better yet,
I could still choose to live alone for the rest of my life.
Who needs a man?

ANN EVERETT

We introduced ourselves, both of us uncomfortable.
I managed to eat my lasagna with only the tiniest speck
of tomato sauce on my all white outfit.
Who wears white to eat Italian?
The conversation was hesitant at times
but not uncomfortable.
Mr. Blue-plaid-shirt did ask me out for a second date.
I was not rejected! I was a single, dating woman.

Our second date was a long drive through Wichita.
Before he left, I walked him to his car.
Each of us stood awkwardly
until he said, "Come here."
I had wondered how it would feel
to be held by this giant of a man.
Would he have a crushing grip
or would I suffocate against his large chest?
I found safe haven in his gentle embrace.

The second date continues until death do us part.
Mr. Blue-Plaid-Shirt?
He no longer has a blue, plaid shirt.

IMPATIENT
For Bob

I sighed—*waiting to be loved;*
come passion's sweep—
no time to sleep.

Memory boxes lined my mind
like dusty coffins filled with joy,
heartache, sighs. All past.

Then he ambled into my world,
gave so much and asked so little.
New memory boxes—
small hopes to test.

He stayed. I have no idea why.
The strength of him lined
mind showcases with sweet touches,
glee, and conversation as best can be.

I took his hand and let him lead
until I found my strength again.
This gentle man did not complain.

I took his hand.
We shared the lead.

ANN EVERETT

THERE WAS MASADA

She stood,
> a grain of sand blown up from the desert,
> rooted in dryness and stone,
> swaying on the plateau rim.

Thirsty,
> she drank in Zealots
> the way greedy lungs move air
> or enlarged pupils dissolve light.

Later,
> at the King David Hotel,
> the man she no longer loved
> slept in their bed.

She sat
> in discomfort on a toilet lid
> in a too-bright bath writing
> *My Masada lies in ruin...*

Emotions,
> swallowed by the decades, taught her
> Masada, the horror, the suffering
> were not about her.

BYLINES 'ROUND THE EYES

The discarded lover
      faded from memory
      long before her poem lines,
      fifty-eight words punctuated by pity.

Masada,
      like a pearl in oyster flesh,
      lodged inside her skull,
      unpolished by time.

Note: After the first Jewish-Roman war, Roman Empire troops surrounded Masada. The Jewish rebels living on Masada preferred death to surrender and slavery. The Rebels set fire to their belongings, then chose ten people by lot to kill everyone else before committing suicide.

ANN EVERETT

SANDMAN

Cranium reverie
lead me languid and mellow
into the journey of illusive imagery.
Blend sky azures with sea greens,
coral reds with dolphin grays.
Whip smooth the dusk by churn of sleep,
sand to glass—
tidal pools whirling toward black impasse.

ADVENT

Advent is catching our breath
and feeling the moment—
something wonderful is about to happen.

Remember record players?
A seventy-eight placed inside a well-worn,
portable box begins to spin.
Poised to dance, we wait for the needle to drop.

When the flavor and scent of song
fill the head with resonance,
we wait for the piano intro to stop.
Melodies will fill our inner spaces.

Our dog looks expectantly out the window,
his whole body wiggling behind a nose
pressed to glass, his eyes wide and bright.
The key in the lock will open his world
to embraces and praise.

Advent is the I-am-ready-to-dance-sing-
embrace-the-world days. Our responsibility?
Dance with lonely souls,
release a carol in a cold, smelly, diminished place,
give a hug to the hard to love. Advent given.

No property is more valuable
to the soul than the belief that
something wonderful is about to happen.

ANN EVERETT

BYLINES 'ROUND THE EYES

MUSIC

ANN EVERETT

JAZZ

i can lie
  in my head
    on the silk
      sheets of sound
i'm the sax
  metal cold
    searched by hands
      feeling gold
valves release
  sounds escape
    improvised
      notes on fire
tongue on reed
  speak to me
    wordlessly
      openly
made to dance
  ev'ry pore
    and my ears
      blue notes see
oh the force
  of the rush
    on the silk
      sheets of sound

ANN EVERETT

THE ORGAN

the organ sounds like
the pound of spring winds against stained glass
the stomp of grapes in alter vats
the tidal roar of miked sermons
the whisper above creaking pews
a Canadian Geese Jack-in-the Box
the dirge tick of perfect time
the rattle of old bones by trumpet's blast
the consolation of a flute breathing velvet
the sigh of death
the chiming of silverware at Thanksgiving
a child's laugh during pew-aisle tag
rain drum-drum-drumming
locus prayers
the heat of desire as thighs touch
perfume invading the mind's pallet
soulful blues against hope
a righteous march by beating hearts
life being lived

HERE COMES J. D.
For J. D. Lehner

The four-foot-something cowboy
wore a coal black, man-sized, felt hat.
Between the brim and fire red shirt
was a face too knowing for a child.

Heat glued us to pews and
salt-tide oozed through feverish skin.
A man behind me whispered,
"Hell can't be much hotter than this."

A cappella, o'er the mike came
a loosened Pascagoula squirrel.
Ray Stevens, move over;
here comes J. D.

ANN EVERETT

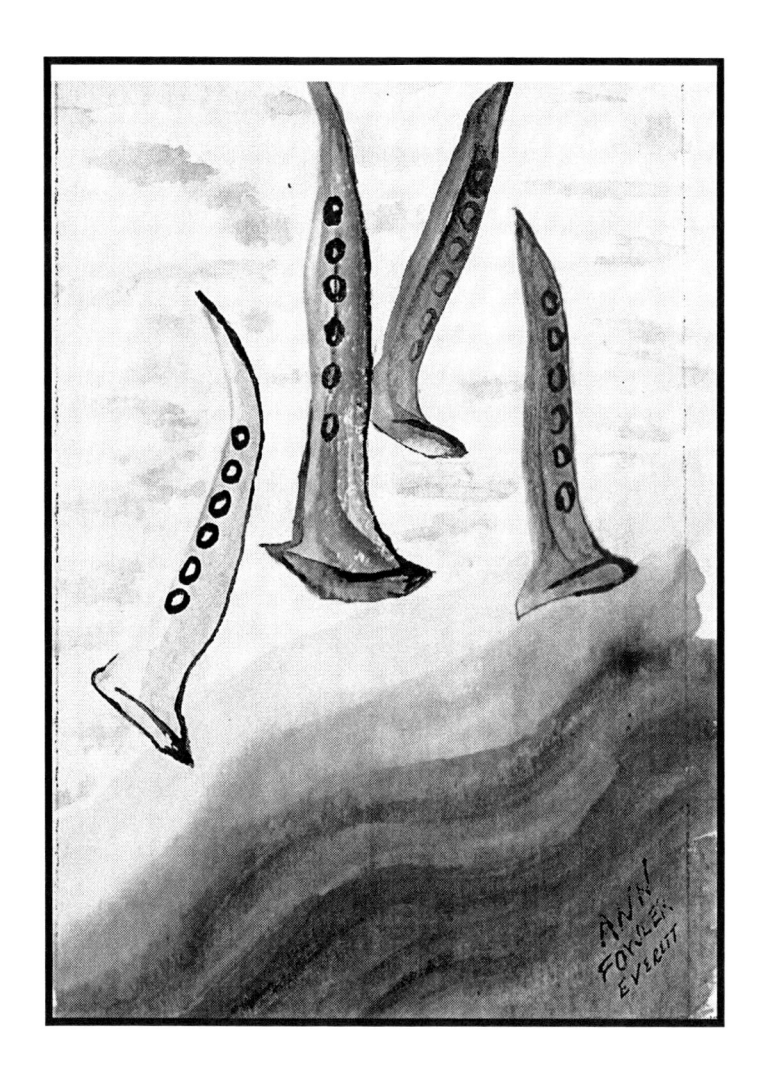

KLEZMER

Ride the clarinet's shrill phrase
beyond lyrics;
soar inward,
soar inward.

The licorice stick speaks
to ears on the ground,
eyes studying storm clouds,
arms bound to the chest, and
a mouth caught
in the ah-h-h-h of the moment.

Barbed wire bedded in satin
does not scratch the flesh—
history composed as an arpeggio,
pain written as melodies in counterpoint.

Women in black pass skirts awhirl;
old men bend toward boys
making roads in the dirt.

Music instructs the silence—
honey on bland biscuits,
angels at our dying.

***Klezmer is Balkans, blues, ancient Jewish culture, history and jazz. Klezmer combines the minor key and an uplifting beat.

ANN EVERETT

HIS FIRST SOLO
For Nathan Moore October 25, 1992

Play a song on your recorder,
lively highs and largo lows,
haunting flute tones, melodies.

May your songs someday inspire
mourners, brides, loved ones, peers.
See our pride in your potential.

QUESTIONING

ANN EVERETT

THE AFFECTED
(Written after the Oklahoma City bombing)

I want to know who steals innocence
from cradled babes and decent folk.
From me. From me. From me.

Surely, the molding of a terrorist
did not come from *Good Night, Moon*
a thousand times read before sleep.

Did he idly finger plush teddy bears
sharing his pillow in night light glow?

Would his dad throw underhand balls
to a blue-striped, little league uniform?

Was the someday terrorist part of a team?
Any team?

Did he laugh at "knock knock" jokes,
play peek-a-boo or hide and seek?

Did he spit watermelon seeds at his sister,
tattle on his brother, or attend family reunions?

ANN EVERETT

The instant a stranger's child dies,
I share one emotion with the terrorist—rage.
Forever outrage.

How then do we take rage and make change?
How do we take the white sheets
draped over the dead
and make white flags of peace?

Peace will come when
all children have a dream,
all dreams find reality,
all reality is safe.

A CONVERSATION WITH KINGS

You rest an eternity in El Escorial Pantheon,
a grand conclusion for Spanish Kings,
the final reign over gold leaf and marble,
an eventuality set by lineage rather than deeds.

Is the Monasterio less cold than entombment
near olive trees and grape vines,
condiments and wine for populous and Kings?
The Costa Del Sol would be warmer—
simply not fitting, too New World chic,
too far from tapestries, painted ceilings,
silk wall coverings and the throne room.

Here you lie, giving unwilling audience to tourists,
a postcard picture in a sweaty child's hand.
To be entombed as an archive,
the subject of weary tour guides,
must give you pause.

ANN EVERETT

In Granada a woman lays flowers
on her Father's grave,
a tear stain on her cheek,
a tremble with each flash of memory.
Near the Mediterranean,
a man casts his wife's ashes into the wind;
the ash touches the olive tree, feeds the sunflower,
brushes against the long-dried,
dark masterpieces in the Prado,
and revisits an old lover.

You are left with echoes on marble
and a cleaning crew to stroke your casket.

Note: El Escorial, NW of Madrid, functions as a
monastery, royal palace, museum and school. It has
been the burial site for most Spanish Kings for the past
five centuries.

IN THE BEGINNING

Energy released static b
                r
              a
              n
              c
            h
              e
            s
                        into the void;
Energy drew a circle,
widening and narrowing,
widening and narrowing,
until the whorl of friction became the first star.
Furnace gasses exploded lava from its center;
lava to harden into red planets, gray moons,
and more suns inside galaxies.

Water fell and craters filled.
Lightening over slime-lined ponds
and new algae created the first ameba
swimming near grasses by water's edge.
Creatures came to slide on their bellies,
crawl on the loam, or
walk barefoot beside the water.
Hearts pulsed.
Beat, beat-beat, beat, beat-beat.

ANN EVERETT

Man was stronger than birds
and smarter than the animals. He ruled.
The lingering, primal fears remained—
the void and lightening.

When black stars collapse in
and return to the beginning of time,
what trails the ashes?
Souls? Time? Memory?

In the beginning was the creator
on the cusp of eternity
longing for beating hearts.
Beat, beat-beat, beat.

BYLINES 'ROUND THE EYES

THIS IS THE WAY IT'S ALWAYS BEEN DONE

"This is the way it's always been done,"
a slogan befitting a bloodied, well-pressed flag
at half mast over shrinking towns, ladies' aids
and dying children on foreign soil.
—expendable local tradesmen
—expendable age diversity
—expendable ethnicity.

Click on the shopping network or order online,
make three, not two or four,
cherry pies for the bake sale,
close weary eyes to images on the world news,
and know you are conscience clear because
"this is the way it's always been done."

ANN EVERETT

THE DICHOTOMY OF GOD AND GODLINESS

The Pharisee wearing the mask of comedy plays
to the mask of drama worn by the conflicted.
        No face.
        Heart place.
Lasers of hell tattoo the landscape—
the heart-tundra within the unforgiven.
        Hunter.
        Hunted.
The black book weighs the law; and
the condemned look to the heavens.
        Judge.
        Accused.
Eternity is pensioned to the ordained;
but, the existential journeyman knows humanity.
        Certainty.
        Uncertainty.
Dichotomies meet in the politics of living.
Dichotomies exist when love fails.
        The lion.
        The lamb.

NOTHING NEW

In a gray high rise home on the wrong side of town
a whore lies on her back, reaching out, pulling down.
At the end of the deal jingles gold, flutters green,
nothing new, nothing real, conscience lean, truth obscene.

In a gray high rise home on the right side of the tracks
meet the lobbyist, businessman, government hacks.
At the end of the deal jingles gold, flutters green,
nothing new, nothing real, conscience lean, truth obscene.

In the gray TV boxes of homes hill and dell
hear the preachers who cry save yourselves from all hell.
At the end of the deal jingles gold flutters green,
nothing new, nothing real, conscience lean, truth obscene.

Note the prostitute, politic, heretic, too;
and the first life defined is most honest and true.
At the end ev'ry deal jingles gold, flutters green,
nothing new, nothing real, conscience lean truth obscene.

ANN EVERETT

THE HOSPITAL GRILL AND DELI

Sandwiched between registration and administration,
the Terrace Grill and Deli waits for visitors descending
from squared, white space. Bones worn sore
by plastic chairs order grilled cheese or salad.
Murmuring families fearing closure
talk beside black mini-blinds.
Where is communion to fill the spirit's belly?

BLUE SHADOWS

Shadows lace snow drifts to stubble;
puddle inside snow angels and rabbit tracks.

Shadows are humble servants
that exist without permission
from seed, architect or creature.
Shadows know what humans have yet to learn—
never wait for permission to grow on a stalk,
build a shell or sway to the music.

Why do we talk of light and not the shadow?
Shadows dance as many steps as the ballerina,
float in concert with clouds
and give sundials merit.

Shadows, in harmony with love, hope and charity,
prove the existence of light.

ANN EVERETT

STALAGTITES

As cavern mists cling fleetingly to swords
in sable suspended so does the creation
hold the creator and the God of light
or darkness breathe in the mind
made soul. Can more
be seen in the glare
than in the liberty
and design of
infinity's
black
hole?

I AM WOMAN
*Written for the Salina District
United Methodist Women 2002*

I am woman:
Scarlet passion, black depression,
yellow joy, cerulean mellow.

I am a woman who loves
the smell of freshly turned earth,
the feel of a baby's pink cheek,
the tastes of apricots and plums.

What color is peace?
What color is God?

I am a woman who loves
to breathe life—
puckered lips releasing
dandelion seeds to the wind,
tight lips in a red face
blowing up balloons,
the quiet lift and release of the chest
as midnight blues fall over sleep.

ANN EVERETT

What color is peace?
What color is God?

I am a woman who loves spring green,
summer garden blooms,
chestnut fall, white winter.

I am a woman who loves the flavors
and monumental celebrations
of the seasons—
strawberries, pumpkin cake,
chocolate Easter bunnies,
birthdays with confetti
and weddings with tears.

What color is peace?
What color is God?

I am a woman who loves.

LAST GOODBYES

ANN EVERETT

A VISIT FROM A STRANGER
For Aunt Mamie Fry 1886-1984

Like my fingerprints on all that I have touched,
I imagine the echoes of my footprints
adhering to the walls and ceiling of the hallway.
Millions of invisible steps,
by virtue of ribbed sound waves,
cling to green paint.

Moans and unintelligible chatter
strike chords on the ivory of my mind,
chords to accompany the rhythm of percussion
heel clinks and the muted scuffs of crepe soles
and rubber tipped walkers.

Wading through a soup
of urine and disinfectant odors,
I carry the weight of my journey until I meet
a wall of big brown eyes, wide and staring
at me as though I am a transparency.
In the fetal position, she rests
in a womb of white taut sheets,
her flesh enmeshed in a woolly, cotton pad.

ANN EVERETT

I search for a way to give her dignity
as once she afforded me worth.
So, I place posters on her walls,
not of paper to be shared by other visitors,
but, of times photographed and
reproduced on glossy memory.

In her gallery I hang a threadbare teddy bear,
the one she mended for me again and again.
Sassafras tea in a china teacup
force a confession, "Aunt Mamie,
I will share my secret;
I hated the taste of sassafras.
Better to drink the tea than risk
never again sharing your special brew."
Tatted lace and tea cups
define the gentle art of her.

Above her bed I place the words
to James Whitcomb Riley's
The Raggedy Man and *The Land of Used-To-Be*.
I thank her for reading poetry to me
when everyone else fed me
The Three Bears and *Cinderella*.

BYLINES 'ROUND THE EYES

A collage displays spool dolls,
a homemade, wooden aggravation board,
Chinese checkers, sock monkeys with big red lips,
Indian dolls, beaded and turquoise jewelry.

Best of all, at chair railing height,
I secure a framed picture
of a long, rumbling, rattling train,
like the one we rode together to Wichita.
I feel the clicks and clanks
of its wheels against the rails,
returning me to the sounds in the hallway.

If someday I entertain strangers by my bed,
I hope they bring portraits of my life
half as brilliant as those I leave with her.

ANN EVERETT

BREASTPLATES
For Janell Rock 1955-2008
A Talented Musician and Recording Artist

Her mind, unshielded by closed lids,
smelled white sheets and uniforms
and felt a needle pour clear lava into her vein,
the mouth of the river named intrusion.
She dared not look
at the cleft each breath raised,
where necklines fell and lovers touched.
Her foot brushed soft linen,
smooth as dirt roads under bike tires—
black glass slick like childhood memory.
As a child she knew who she was—
first and clan names secured her worldly place;
her dreams guaranteed the future.
Wide-eyed she saw the dreams uncorseted.
Vulnerable and unteathered,
her independence stolen by cancer,
her gentle spirit became the ward
of family and friends.

Now, far from pain
and the restraints of disease,
she can ride the eighty-eight keys
in a flurry of jazz renditions.
Heaven's choir must be singin',
shoutin', and gettin' down!

THE CORRIDOR
For Lane Rock 1952-1992
and his mother, Velma Rock, 1920-2009

She cradled in gentle strength a dying son—
wasting, hurting, losing control of walk,
sight, and vocal command.
At last was known the future past tense.

She cooked, sewed, laughed, and masked tears
for the final rally that would usher the genteel son,
companion, brother, friend from life posed on ebb.
She remembered a time when tea and crackers
were served for fever and flu.

The heartless judged and the dying forgave ignorance,
pain, the living for health, and the fallen for surrender.
AIDES, the cannibal, fed on dreams and hope,
and stole the carefree child from his Mother's arms.

ANN EVERETT

GOODBYE
For Aunt Ellen Burwell 1903-1995

Waiting is the heartland soil
you held in hand to plow or seed,
the loam scent sucked into the lungs—
sweet as lilacs blooming,
raw as workshop dust,
strong as saddle blankets' musky smell.

Oh, pioneer woman who farmed in overalls,
your hand-crafted, rocking, wooden horses
carried us a thousand miles;
your hand-tied quilts comforted us at night;
and, your blessings on our peculiarities
branded us with love.
Your persona inspired us to move forward,
care for family, be ourselves.

We reluctantly give you back
to open skies, dry southern winds
and snowdrifts in December.

BYLINES 'ROUND THE EYES

I JUST LOVE YOU
For Freda Reifschneider - November 1998

"I just love you," she said,
the word "love" emphasized.

Her hand clasped mine
and I felt a cradle blanket
tucked under my chin,
the comfort of an adult lap,
a rhythmic rock, a lullaby,
childhood joy reclaimed.

"I just love you," she said,
the word "love" emphasized.

Her words inspired
the better me,
the woman I longed to be—
generous, smiling,
trusting, gentle, confident.

Now, made whole,
she stands firmly above the stars,
sees rainbows with renewed clarity,
listens to the choir,
claps her hands with joy,
and the saints say,

"Freda, we just love you,"
the word "love" emphasized.

ANN EVERETT

THOSE I HAVE KNOWN OR LOVED

ANN EVERETT

CHRISTMAS

For the Herington United Methodist Women

Lighted decorations hang on downtown posts;
snow trims store windows;
Santa heads bob to blinking Rudolf noses;
taped music is caught in list-filled, mind gauze—
    gloves for Sally,
    a tie for Joe,
    a politically correct Barbie for Cindy,
    fresh cranberries,
    canned pumpkin,
    whipping cream.
Christmas hearts glow with the shared history
of programs past—
    the three-year-old who yawned
    and fell of a stack of books,
    the lines memorized and forgotten,
    velvet Christmas dresses,
    halos slipping to the side,
    the child who sang loudest
    and couldn't carry a tune,
    a darkened church,
    lighting the Christ candle.

From the season of purple to the advent of white,
Christmas lives in women's hearts.
Crèche to cross. Crèche to cross.

ANN EVERETT

THE CARETAKER

If I, the poet, could form sentences
to separate my life from his,
place disjointed lessons in stanzas
or make something beautiful of pain,
then I could begin to find
who I have become during his dying,
the dying process of yesterday and tomorrow.
Today……….unspeakable.

The monster, Alzheimer's
slithered lazily into our home,
sat unfed during the long winter,
watched his victim through half-closed eyes,
stroked his fears with his tongue.
The delusions began.
Memory lessened.
My love inched away from me
and sat on the monster's back.

Then the feeding. Slowly at first.
I saw him slip inside the monster's jaws.
I screamed, "Do not leave me."
He told monster tales—
his parents sleeping in our home,
the return of children
and voices speaking from empty rooms.

BYLINES 'ROUND THE EYES

I watched him struggle
against the monster's clenched jaws,
the possession complete, death so far away.
Swallowed whole, his bulk swelled
the belly of the disease.

I was left with the creature.

Something in the creature's smile
reminded me of a man who fed squirrels,
rode free on a motorbike
through Florida orange groves,
knew the forest trees by name,
studied the stars, made love to me
and to the whole of his existence.
So I stayed. I listened for his laugh.

I cared for the disease,
loved and stroked the lump
that represented my husband?
I tended the pain and endured the ranting.
I laid beside the monster at night and
awakened to confusion
in the wee hours of the morning.

I forgot who I am.
Surely this is so,
because I once knew words.
Words are who I am.

ANN EVERETT

PERFECTION

Art is found in perfect imperfection—
rusty windmills spin and compose song bursts;
sea shells dress in the ebbing tide's erosion; and
children spill milk, crumbs, and laughter.
The artist—farmer, beach comber, mother—
stroke, brush, and embrace life.

GRADUATION

My wish for you this day
is more than knowledge born
of study, essay, test;
but, rather comfort worn
by friendship often shown—
yourself, the friend best known.

ANN EVERETT

SKYWRITERS

Hear the jet's roar;
watch the landing gear appear
for a smooth landing at McConnell Air Force Base.
Study the vapor trails,
white streaks to skywrite recent history—
practice runs, men leaving,
women returning home from duty,
or the thrill of a pilot's first flight.

Parents show their children
sheep and sailboats in the clouds—
generation to generation studying the sky.
Lessons in creativity, joy and peace
are taught in those shared moments.
No grander lullaby was ever written
or nightlight better crafted
than bare tree limbs against a full moon.

War mongers do not look at rainbows.
Those who each day fall in love sunrises,
sunset's red light on wheat,
the stars and moon
embrace higher ideals.

To look up, smile, and know beauty
is the peace initiative of the common man.

THE POET'S BAPTISM

Inside the poet is a matrix stirring,
a place more boundless, wild and free
than the least-tame kingdoms,
beasts on prowl, or rituals of pagans.

Lightning behind the eyes
thrusts the poet awake
and casts her into a universe
more vast than those envisioned
by scientist, psychic, or the converted.

Mankind's ahs and ohs strike
as clappers against chimes.
Ink and paper lead the way to the unfolding
of words—melodic phrases
that know no master.

The poet bathes in the hallowed
pools of inspiration.

ANN EVERETT

THE PACT

"Help!"

Bedroom? Bath? Kitchen?
A rushed shuffle.
He mustn't fall before she's found.
His pulse races and cheeks burn.

Inside the bathroom and
on her knees, she waits.
Tears in her eyes are
poignant reminders of dependence.

They cling to one another,
shelved in a condominium,
feebly coordinating everyday tasks,
contemplating the past, denying death.
He hates her for growing old
and himself for allowing it.

Attempts to lift her fail.
He retrieves the stepstool from the kitchen
and his walker from the living room.
Five, ten, twenty minutes pass
before she successfully stands on fragile limbs.
New bruises appear and
both suffer from strained muscles.

The pact: tell no one.

Community agencies and their children
threaten their independence.
They comfort one another
and wait for the next fall.

ANN EVERETT

A TWO-YEAR-OLD CHRISTMAS
For George

He is a two-year-old
who delights with unexpected gifts:
hugs and kisses,
an arm chair sleeve across my shoulder,
dust mitts waving hello from my bed.

He lives in a seventy-eight-year-old body,
Christmas less a calendar event
than a return to his own nativity.

    Nativity: joy in the moment,
                    grief unknown,
                    peace for the price of an oatmeal cookie.

Protective angels, love,
change, joy, and peace,
a graying babe to lead the way
to the crèche of divine humanity.

FAMILY

ANN EVERETT

EIGHTEEN
For My Niece, Sarah

Dreams, night and day,
expose hopes and desires—
riders flung onto kite tails
above mind clouds.

Time—today is forever;
past mistakes lie ahead
far from drifting, drifting
youthful pleasures.

Belief in kites, dreams,
and the promise of tomorrow,
float on unpredictable zephyrs.
No child owns yesterday.

Drifting—how the lesson is taught
to chart and steer the vessel
caught up in breezes
sprung from the heart.

ANN EVERETT

COLLISION COURSE
For My Nephew, Matt

He cruised in darkness, auto set,
one more truck to pass.
Two a.m., coffee fueled,
four hours from home,
he steered straight between white lines
and trusted rules of order.
Truckers on CBs screamed, "Stop!"
Destiny neared. "Stop!" "Stop!"
Landscape hid the woman
traveling wrong way on four-lane.
Liquor through her veins pulsed;
amber drenched gray matter—
reason lost to triples.
On an incline and feeling each set-'m-up-Joe,
she pressed the gas pedal against the floorboard.
Like glitter on pavement, glass shattered,
rooted in hair and slashed flesh.
The spleen burst and jaw shattered,
consciousness lost.
Metal screamed angry, shrill sounds, and
wrapped humans inside steel cocoons.
Rubber marked passages
of cars and mortal bodies.
Sorrows drowned met innocence—
two lives forever changed.

ANGEL WINGS
For Tiffany

On her shoulders lay
a white, Pilgrim collar—
like collapsed angel wings.
Nine-year-old Tiffany glows
as she waits for time to pass,
for her turn to present dialogue
in her first school play.
Eyes widen above her debut
in blush and lipstick,
the smile as eager as spring water
rushing into pools of light.
Her hands raise the white collar
to the jaw line; then the torso
collapses onto a nervous body.
Tiffany holds excitement
the only way a child can—
kinetic frenzy dancing
to a unique rhythm all her own.
Feet shuffle,
pores open to stage air,
soul and sprite paired
to waltz through the night.

Oh, the magic of light and microphone,
costume and script;
the enchantment of Tiffany
cloaked in angel wings.

ANN EVERETT

WINTER STORM
For My Father

Snowflakes dissolved on his blush;
eyes closed under an uneven hairline;
the worn, hand-me-down jacket
tightly bound arms to torso.

      "Come here, son."

Nine-year-old lungs inhaled cold air;
the heartbeat quickened and eyes reopened.
Retracing his footprint trail, toe to heel,
he neared the smell of gingerbread.

      "Take off your wet socks."

The loosened shoe strings testified
his rush to play rather than endure
the ritual of laces twice looped.
The thud of shoes and fall of clay stained socks
undressed numb feet.

      "Here, put these on."

He shrank inside his Dad's gray, knitted work socks
pulled from the stove-side rack.
"If only Christmas could come
more than just one day a year,"
he bargained, "I'd give up dreaming during school
and not squirm in church…least not much."

ANN EVERETT

"You're old enough to know…."

The socks pulled to his knees comforted him.
Mom took his hands. Her stare he refused to meet.
The taste of yellow and green rose to his throat and
he tried to close his ears to the disclosure of whatever
he was old enough to know.

"There is no Santa Clause."

He willed vinegar tears back into unilluminated sockets,
back into a wounded spirit,
back behind the trust given his parents.
From the betrayer of his belief,
he reclaimed his hands and his heart swept clear
joy, peace, hope and, yes, even love.

"Son, you had to be told this year."

Feet, drowning in Dad's socks,
were stuffed into wet shoes.
"If you lied about Santa, then there's no God either!"
At Christmas his dreams came true for a short time—
he knew he was special because Santa remembered
all deserving girls and boys.

"My darling boy, I love you."

A parent's love wasn't the same.
Parents stuck with ugly,
stupid or mean children still managed to love them.
No, only Santa and God loved lost
and lonely girls and boys, the spiritual proof of worth.
Dignity dissolved as the snow puddled under his shoes.

    "Put your coat on before you go out to play."

Gingerbread men mocked him with beady eyes
and big, red, all-knowing smiles. He slammed the door
on innocence and on the truth he knew in his dreams.
Rage spilled from spleen and bowels.
A young man swallowed iced air and the child vanished.

ANN EVERETT

I HOLD MY BREATH
For Tiffany

Drowning in my fear,
I watch Tiffany jump into the water,
ten feet reaching up to pull her down,
the splash a resounding eulogy.

I suck air into my lungs,
holding it for her,
waiting for the nine-year-old to surface.
Too much time passes.

I cannot hold my breath any longer.

She's disappeared and I freeze.
Tearing, I'm anguished
by the lifeguard's preoccupation
with a teen wearing an inviting grin
larger than her bikini.

I'll dive in after Tiffany—
better I drown in an attempt to save her
than live knowing I allowed her to die
for the thrill of a plunge.

BYLINES 'ROUND THE EYES

She reappears at the pool's edge
after an easy underwater swim,
climbs the ladder and smiles.
Perched on her suit's bodice,
Tweety confirms her identity.
I return her smile.

She walks quickly to the diving board line,
the long strides invented to avoid
the humiliation of a lifeguard's whistle,
a public scolding for the sin of running.
She waits her turn at the diving board and
jumps into the pool.

I hold my breath.

ANN EVERETT

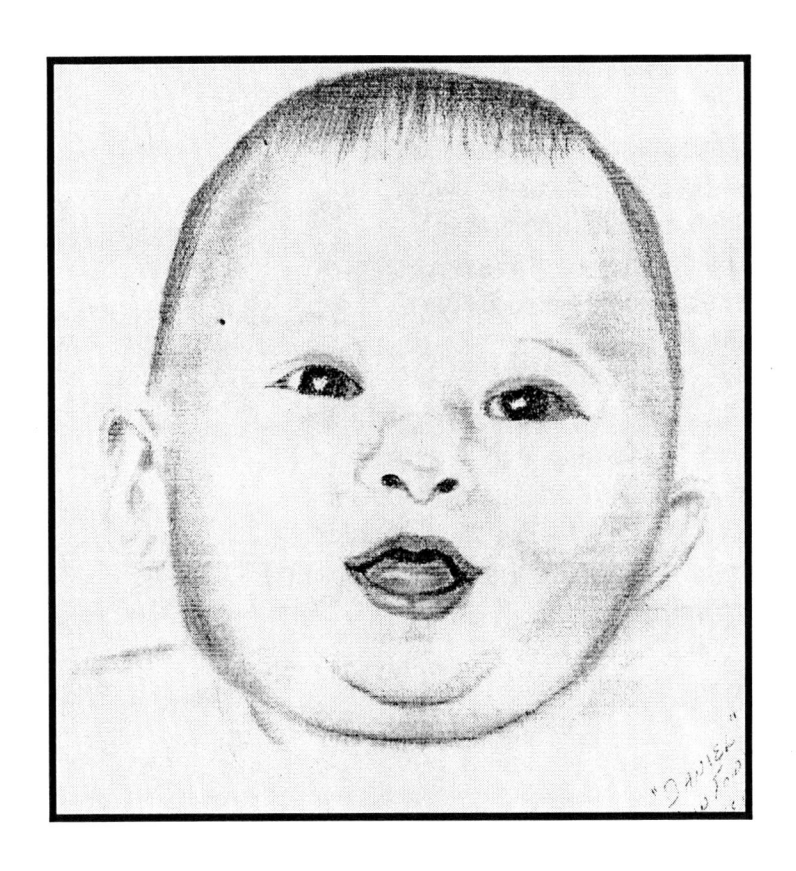

UNCONDITIONAL LOVE
For Michelle and Daniel

Dark hair swept over her face
the way eagle wings brush sky,
silent art in motion,
solitude on a cloud canvas.

She eased across gold bed covers,
resting on elbows and pelvis,
head lowered over her first born,
in love with his smell,
the taste of ten grasping fingers,
the feel of infant flesh stilled for sleep,
and the coos—love songs composed
by a gifted son for his mother.

She was the child of parents
who wore neediness like a choker
three sizes too small, a thick leather strap
catching laughter in the chest
and love's breath inside a tightened rib cage
until marriage bonds suffocated.

She searched for what she did not know—
the unconditional, the forever, an absolute.
Within her grew a miracle,
more than babe of DNA chains,
larger than her best fantasy.
She birthed the child who gave her life.

ANN EVERETT

HERITAGE WEB
For Jeff

Under the ageless Florida sun
cabbage palm fronds rustled
and an insect symphony accompanied
Jeff, age three, on safari hunting spiders.
Inside the stucco house his grandfather
gently captured spiders on the Orlando Sentinel
and carried them from the house
saying, "Spiders gotta live, too."
Library books opened to tarantulas,
black widows, brown recluses,
and "itsy, bitsy spider."

At age eleven Jeff searched heaven's web—
stars, black holes, asteroids and planets,
the world of Carl Sagan and Stephen Hawking.
He dreamed of rockets, moon walks, and space travel,
interests parallel with his grandfather
who watched Cosmos and read incessantly.

In the universe of blood,
Jeff lived ancestral dreams and enjoyed
the intellect of inherited, genetic codes.
Not unlike the webs of spiders
or orbit of the heavens,
Jeff walked the silken lines nature dictated—
a new star shining in the universe of family.

MOTHER

ANN EVERETT

FINDING VOICE

Between my Father's death and burial,
my Mother told this story to her grandchildren.

Eva and I did laundry using a ringer washing machine
and two, four-legged, rinse tubs.
Hung on wire lines wiped clean,
white, bleached sheets hid cotton underwear.

Herbert, my brother and a newlywed,
came to visit daddy.
Modesty prevented us from ringing bras flat
or hanging them out to dry.

We busied ourselves with mending until Herbert left,
then rushed to the porch and to the cistern water
long soaking personal garments.

We lifted the first knotted bra from the tub;
then the second, third and fourth.
I could imagine the smile on Herbert's face—
a new way to torment little sisters.

Eva and I never told daddy what Herbert did—
too embarrassing to repeat.
I miss Eva and Herbert—daddy, too.

While waiting to see my Father's body,
completely silent and groomed by strangers,
I listened to her tale
and strange connections in her voice—
love, life, death, bras, today, yesterday.

ANN EVERETT

THE SPICE SHUFFLE

I sit between Bob and Mother,
Jack the beagle at my feet;
Mother reaches over with her white-socked foot,
rubs jack's back, and visibly relaxes.

She quickly plays the Skip Bo cards in her hand:
one, Skip Bo, three, four, Skip Bo.
With great satisfaction
she plays the six from her stack—
one play closer to a win.
Bob calls her "Skippy."
I say, "Go, girl, go!"
The ninety-year-old rises up in her chair
and enjoys the momentary success.

At the card table Mother's spirit is larger
than her fragile skeleton and parchment skin.
She drums the table as if responding
to the demands of her pianist hands.
Her frame adjusts and readjusts on the chair pad,
an oversized pillow at her back.

BYLINES 'ROUND THE EYES

Cards are more than a deck of numbers.
Cards bring out the true character of a person—
the ranter, the shy bidder, the take-no-prisoners player,
the intellectual, the resigned, the humorist, and
the I-have-a-captive-audience talker.
Each hand is a new opportunity to succeed or fail,
take risks or play it safe, and
enjoy the comfort of company—a game of life.

What is family? What is holy? What inspires us?
Spices of conversation, family,
and love around the kitchen table.

ANN EVERETT

BEHIND THE LINES

"The nurse told me to throw
all the old ones away,"
she said. Her defiance
drew lines around her mouth.
      DEEP LINES.
Out of her purse she produced
a two-inch stack of yellowed cards.
"I can give you my blood pressure
and weight for many years past."
      RIGID LINES.
"Nineteen-eighty-four. M-m-m-m-m.
Blood pressure one-forty over eighty."
Her small frame lifts,
the chin cemented upward.
      STRAIGHT LINES.
"Why am I keeping them?
Because the nurse at the Senior Center
told me to throw MY cards away!"
She shuffled the cards with her thumb.
      DRAWN LINES.
Retucked in a dark, purse pocket,
the cards waited to be whipped
before the nurse's nose as casually
as a tissue or a grandchild's photo.
      A RED ROVER LINE.

CIRCLE OF LIFE

Long ago I watched Mother primp
before a mirror edged with worn silvering .

Summer light played against dark curls,
the sculpt of her cheekbones,
and the luminescent shine of red lips.

Shorter than the wash basin,
I studied her grooming ritual—
fingers stroked the rouge jar and then her cheeks;
the powder puff dulled the canvas of her face.
In small hands the hair brush detangled
and arranged tresses newly shaped by a home perm.

No one ever looked more beautiful.

Mother, now ninety, lives in our home.
Short, gray hair crowns her fragile frame.
When Mother's eyes sparkle with a smile and greeting,
I remember the light of that summer morning.

ANN EVERETT

WOMEN'S AND CHILDREN'S ISSUES

ANN EVERETT

THE PRICE OF BREAD

A vehicle chokes on fuel and age,
angst expelled in a burned-fossil-cloud.

From Windows '07 to the window pane,
I refocus, connect the shines of car doors
and children—images less smooth
than the geometric doodles of my screen saver.
My elbows rest on bulging folders
of food and utility vouchers.
In my overfed self, I perch,
wait for her to near,
wait to digest her pain.

I study her clothes—
the sandals sold for a quarter at the church's closet,
a faded, too-tight tee, and threadbare jeans,
not unlike designer jeans intentionally slit at the knees.
Her children appear as accessories,
part of the ensemble,
one on the hip and one held by the hand.

ANN EVERETT

I see the dread in her eyes,
she must cant the details of her poverty,
her failures, her children's hunger.
I host the coerced confessional,
each intimate detail recorded in a folder for an eternity,
the litany required to feed her children,
to continue heat and water.

Hope has always flown on the wind
and in comet tail glow,
in the certainty that things could change.
Civilized, we fly hope on vouchers,
statistics and political rhetoric.

The shame of poverty.

The shame of charity.

DEPRESSION

How many minute pieces of her stuck
to crepe soles,
to freshly-lacquered hair,
to grime centered under revolving doors,
to discarded, chocolate covered cherry boxes,
to city lamp poles and country fence posts?

Shattered by too many vagrant hands
fondling her fragile soul,
her jack hammered self
bled into powdered microscopic bits of being—
the inarticulate body of a village child.

Two, thirty-two or eighty-two,
a dustpan baby rides time
until love lessons sweep the remnants
into palaces, cathedrals, and waiting arms.

ANN EVERETT

LOVE CHILDREN

Love children—
homeless children who smell of the street,
the bully who learned from his abuser,
the hungry with swollen stomachs,
laughing babes on swings,
the imp hiding a book and flashlight under bed covers,
foster children who no longer attach to anyone,
children victimized by sex peddlers,
children who long to be perfect,
children who believe they are unlovable,
children on ballpark fields,
children practicing for music lessons,
children holding art brushes,
children who do or do not complete their chores,
boys with frogs,
girls with dolls,
children who swim with fish,
children who laugh at their own jokes,
the child nursed at the breast,
the child lifted onto the shoulders of dad.

A WOMAN'S COMMUTE INTO THE CITY

```
    riding waves            in the pool of night
  a school of lights    floats        on the horizon
 bare            coral limbs         pull in the dawn
 streams of headlamps        greet         and pass
 and form a long        red         broken        tail
             from hills           to plains
                 night         to light
           fantasy shapes     sharpen into reality
     baring the teeth     of architect      and engineer
   the city        closes its jaws          on the traveler
```

ANN EVERETT

WAIT HERE

Wait here.
      Where?
      In the dark?
Rest your head
on my shoulder.
      Wait here.
      I want
      to play.
I'll walk my hand
up your ribs.
Wait here.
      Knock, knock.
      Who's there?
The man
in the moon.
Wait here.
      Man in the
      moon who?
Who rapes
the night.
Wait here.

SILENT SCREAMS

She swallowed a totem.
Flesh—a porous veneer
over caved memory—hardened;
indigestible features in silent recall
narrowed her breathing;
the face she wore

—next to her heart—

wondered why valves beat
beyond the death of sleep;
stomach juices churned and
the rancid breath of truth screamed,

I am the abused child of yesterday
and the angry face you see.
She swallowed a totem.

ANN EVERETT

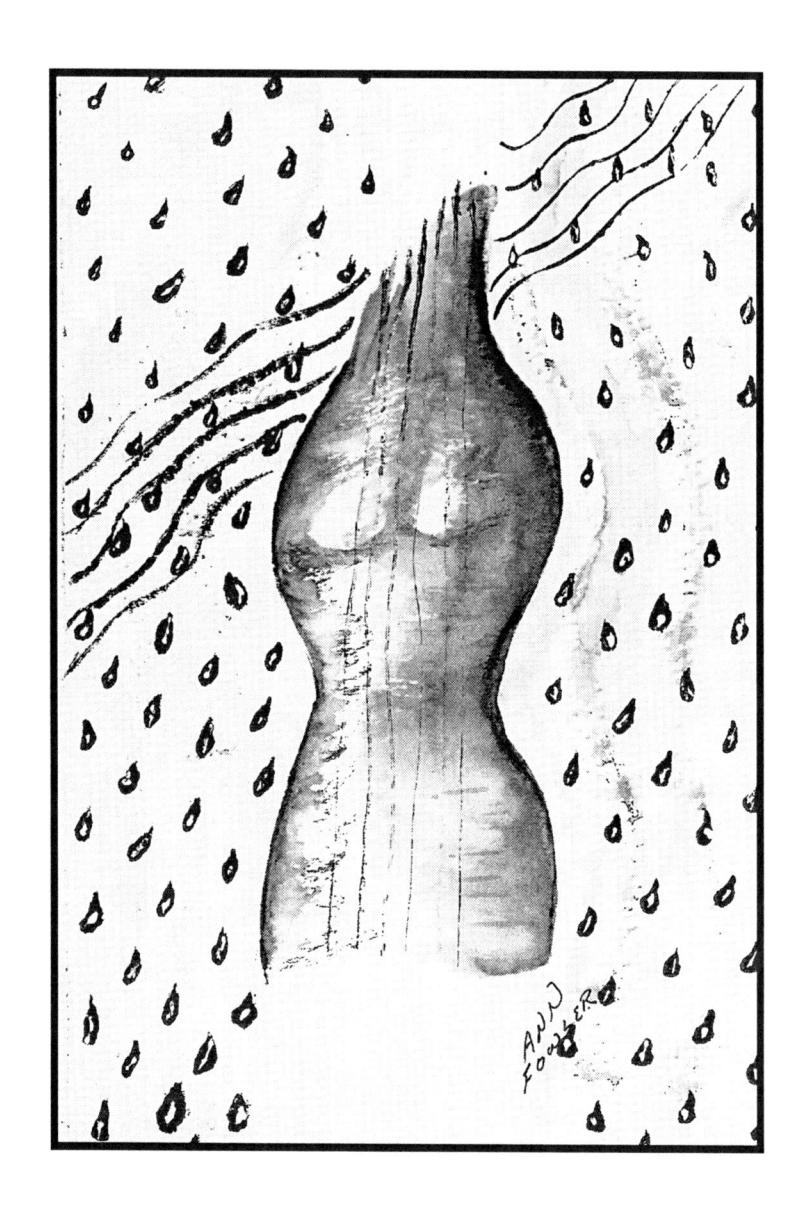

BAGATELLE

She allowed him
to play her
like strings
on a vintage guitar.

He stroked sounds
above veneers.
From dark, empty spaces
vibrations moved her.

When he left,
she was the same—
an instrument
waiting for his touch.

ANN EVERETT

FROM A FORTY-NINE PLYMOUTH

He fumbled with petite, four-hole buttons
and the hooks on a thirty-four B bra;
    the back seat of a blue, forty-nine Plymouth
    smelled musty like soured rain or sex;
"We haven't space enough," she said
as her blouse opened and legs parted.

Inside her a child grew,
not of his dreams or her longings;
    above the stomach
    bulge she cried,
"I haven't space enough
for me and you inside."

The threesome shared a third floor walk-up.
She bought day old bread and mended clothes
    and nightly walked a crying child
    until she knew it was over;
"There's not space enough
for what I feel inside this marriage."

Her bag was packed before noon.
A neighbor watched the child
    as she boarded a train
    for New York City.
There won't ever
be space enough.

REBECCA
(The first transsexual in a small town)

She was too much stalk,
like protea or milkweed.
The voice worn low in her belly
stopped ears with wax of prejudice.

Few touched her;
no one saw her center
before the death
of a beautiful bloom.

ANN EVERETT